The SAZERAC

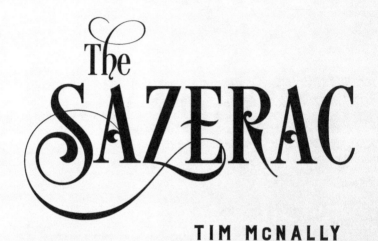

The
SAZERAC

TIM McNALLY

St. John the Baptist Parish Library
2920 New Hwy. 51
LaPlace, LA 70068

LOUISIANA STATE UNIVERSITY PRESS
BATON ROUGE

Published with the assistance of the Borne Fund

Published by Louisiana State University Press
www.lsupress.org

Manufactured in the United States of America
First printing

Designer: Barbara Neely Bourgoyne
Typeface: Arno Pro
Printer and binder: Integrated Book International (IBI)

Cover image: LightFieldStudios/istockphoto.com
Title page image and photo on page xii: Courtesy Sazerac Company

Library of Congress Cataloging-in-Publication Data
Names: McNally, Tim, author.
Title: The Sazerac / Tim McNally.
Description: Baton Rouge : Louisiana State University Press, 2020. |
    Includes bibliographical references.
Identifiers: LCCN 2020002976 | ISBN 978-0-8071-7166-0 (cloth)
Subjects: LCSH: Cocktails—Louisiana—New Orleans—History. |
    Alcoholic beverages—Louisiana—New Orleans. | LCGFT: Cookbooks.
Classification: LCC TX951 .M348 2020 | DDC 641.87/40976335—dc23
LC record available at https://lccn.loc.gov/2020002976

To my wife, my life companion, my mentor, my teacher, my life preserver, my path through the forest, my counselor, and my greatest supporter, Brenda. You have taken me to places of the heart and mind that, on my own, I would never have found or even have known existed.

CONTENTS

ACKNOWLEDGMENTS

My parents, Harold and Lois, were wonderful people. They were not flashy, nor did they live an exciting lifestyle, at least not by the standards I would now consider as such. But they were decent, honest, and dedicated to their families and their four sons. Exceedingly kind and fair, they instilled in us the tools we needed to become quality contributors to the society in which we would likely spend our lives.

Thanks to Father Wilson at St. Monica Catholic Church in Dallas, who counseled an eighth-grade schoolboy not to enter the seminary until after high school. Such sage advice has never been forgotten. Thanks also to many teachers at Jesuit High School in Dallas who taught the importance of how to think rather than what to think.

To Gerald Kindal, a runaway Englishman relocated to a French town masquerading as an American city, thank you for lighting the fire about wine and its infinite iterations and pleasures.

I am indebted to Dale DeGroff and the artistically talented Jyl DeGroff, who turned the world toward quality cocktails, properly constructed, with balance and grace, which is applicable to the drink and their kind friendship.

So many more people deserve recognition, but if I go on, I will surely overlook good friends whose love has enlightened my time on this earth.

Still, I cannot fail to mention the enchanting, glorious, always-full-of-surprises City of New Orleans. She has been welcoming, accepting, enterprising, and challenging. For more than fifty years, I have given no serious thought to living anywhere else. I do not regret that lack of creative direction one little bit.

The
SAZERAC

Introduction

I am not quite sure of the date when I had my first encounter with the cocktail named Sazerac, but I am quite certain where it was and what was the occasion.

The Friday before Mardi Gras in New Orleans is a time of great celebration. In New Orleans, great celebrations are not "sometimes" things. They are "all the time" things. But the Fridays before Mardi Gras and Christmas are two times when holding back is not part of the plan. On both days, office workers, families, social organizations, and people just looking for a good party let it all hang out. Those designations, by the way, include everyone. The madness includes plenty of adult beverages, lots of fine food, music, and general craziness. All are the orders of the day.

I am fortunate enough to be invited each year to a grand celebration staged by the participants on two floats for the Hermes parade. On this occasion, my longtime friend and frequent tennis partner Tony Zanki invited me to a private room at Antoine's Restaurant in the French Quarter, where thirty or so pillars of New Orleans society gathered to renew long-standing friendships, swap stories of past Carnivals and parades, dine together on filet mignon and soufflé potatoes, and begin the drinking of old-fashioneds, manhattans, Sazeracs, and all manner of wines.

Very dressy affair with suits, ties, and fresh haircuts. Hermes is one of the more traditional marching organizations, having staged its first parade, always at night the Friday before Mardi Gras, in 1937—an odd moment in history, between a Great Depression and another world war, to start an elaborate parading organization intent on celebrating a French Catholic, slightly pagan festival. From the beginning of Hermes, the traditions of Carnival, dating to the 1860s, were respected. Today's floats for the parade still, for the most part, make use of the original caissons, the rolling structures on which the floats are built, upgraded and retrofitted to accommodate the changes in parade style that have occurred over more than eighty years.

One of the "grown-up" traditions at the luncheon is to have a drink that is not your normal tipple. For me, that was a Sazerac. The combination of Antoine's historic surroundings, founded in 1840 and still operated by the same family to this day; a bunch of great guys devoted to upholding Carnival tradition and having a fine time; steak and soufflé potatoes; Baked Alaska; and fine cocktails properly made, all intoxicating in themselves. Magic.

The Sazerac tied it all together, and for years, I enjoyed a lone Sazerac only at the Hermes luncheon. Seemed appropriate and proper. Did not seem as if the drink would work as well in August.

Then the craze settled over us. The Sazerac cocktail rediscovered became perfectly acceptable whenever. The challenge with the Sazerac was that it is a particular style of drink, not only defined by its ingredients but also by its construction.

It's true, sometimes even when I am traveling outside of New Orleans, that the drink does receive its proper respect. "Do you want a gin and tonic, a rum and Coke, or a Sazerac?" Drink choices do not work that way in my mind. Sort of like looking at an authentic riverboat powered by steam and figuring out where to put the sauna.

The amazing part of a Sazerac is that the cocktail has survived since the middle 1800s, morphed with the times, and retained its sense of history while becoming modern. Along the way, it has spun off other cocktails, influenced lives, participated in the story of American westward expansion, proudly bragged about its Caribbean roots, and played the role of a critical additive at important and fun times.

Even when the imbiber is not a particularly enthusiastic fan of a specific ingredient and changes to the recipe are made, there is still respect for the drink's name, and a new name is applied to the alternative beverage. Popular cocktails like the old-fashioned, the whiskey cocktail, and the manhattan are branches of the Sazerac family tree.

I've now become more realistic in the frequency of my Sazerac lust. It's no longer just a Carnival treat. But I have not compromised on my beliefs about how the drink should be made and what ingredients are essential, assuming the name of the drink is going to remain "Sazerac." We must all agree that this particular drink is made in a particular way, with particular ingredients. Anything else can be called something else. It's sort of like visitors calling the name of my city "N'Awluns." Not cool and never right.

RAISON D'ÊTRE

My intention here is to share the story of the Sazerac cocktail, including the times in which it was born and has existed for almost two hundred years. I give particular emphasis to the multiple and diverse ingredients that have been a part of the Sazerac cocktail during its lifetime. The whole of the final product is better than the sum of its parts, but the parts are quite interesting in their own right.

CHAPTER ONE

The Beginnings
A PERSPECTIVE

Our in-depth understanding of the historical period of the late 1700s is, at best, muddled and confused. The Western world was recovering from revolution and in the throes of sorting matters out. America had revolted against the tyranny of an incompetent ruler, George III of England. This monarch's awkward treatment of his subjects across the Atlantic Ocean has been partially blamed on a mental condition brought on by a blood disease, porphyria, which causes aches, pains, and blue urine. Such physical ailments are understandably going to mess up a mind. In this case, they likely did just that.

Unlike so many rumors of history, this story seems to be true. The urine hue could have been caused by medications, but the man did indeed exhibit intermittent signs of madness, and his subjects in the American colonies were not amused or entertained. Even loyalists on both sides of the Atlantic had difficulty justifying the king's edicts and tax increases.

Across the English Channel, the monarchy in France was not faring much better. King Louis XVI was the ruler during a time of public unrest brought on by constant wars, profligacy in government spending, social disconnection between a monarch and his subjects, poor harvests, and a royal court populated by incompetent ministers. Within both France and England, the news and the stories of the success of the unfolding American Revolution only encouraged a difficult situation to become worse.

So what we commonly know of this historical period is primarily of crowns being overturned and riots in both

Europe and America. The inner workings of the courts in both England and France are not fully disclosed nor fully understood by historians.

From this period, there was an outgrowth of democracy and innovation. The rise of American leaders and the militarily successful populist but elitist Napoleon brought about the changes the populations were seeking in governance and lifestyle. As old ways were being violently kicked out, there was an enthusiastic openness to the "new" from "the people," who were not accustomed to being masters of their own fate or even having a say in governance.

Freedom is a mighty but unwieldy sword.

It was easy in an era of big ideas and big events to overlook seemingly minor developments. There was, interestingly, a very small item in a Hudson, New York, Federalist newspaper, *Balance and Columbian Repository,* on May 13, 1806, responding to a reader's question, "What is a cocktail?" This inquiry indicates the term *cocktail* was entering into society's general use before 1806, but this was the first reference in print to the phenomenon. The newspaper's answer was, in typical language of the day, convoluted and not to the point: "A cock-tail, then, is a stimulating liquor composed of spirits of any kind—sugar, water, and bitters—it is vulgarly called a Bittered Sling and is supposed to be an excellent electioneering potion, inasmuch as it renders the heart stout and bold, at the same time that it fuddles the head. It is said, also to be of great use to a Democratic candidate: because, a person having swallowed a glass of it, is ready to swallow anything else." And there you have it, a new term without reference to origin. And all connected to a negative remark about a political party. That part does not seem to have changed very much in our modern times.

Authors today such as Dale DeGroff, Ted Haigh, and David Wondrich have built on common knowledge in reporting on adult beverages from ages past. Their and others' search for quotable material about cocktails through the 1800s turned up mostly oral folktales and only a few written references. For over two hundred years, speculation has run rampant about where the term *cocktail* originated. One of the stories even surmised that New Orleans was ground zero for the term, expanding the explanation to a food preparation accessory, the French eggcup—*coquetier*—used to mix a drink's ingredients after breakfast. Americans, it was conjectured, had trouble pronouncing the name of the French dish and ultimately bastardized the name to "cocktail." While this is a wonderful conjecture and somebody went to a great deal of mental acrobatics to explain the origin of the term, it does not likely match up with the timing of the eggcup story during the late 1700s.

There was also the scholarly explanation that the early mixed drinks were stirred with the tailfeather of a rooster, or cock. Even if the stirring had taken place in this manner, it is unlikely that the now well-mixed beverage would take its name from the stir stick, a feather.

Today we have settled on the latest suggestion that innkeepers of the late 1700s bought their spirits in casks. That is true. At the end of the cask's life, there were still spirits in the cask, but this residue was not easily removed. The "tailings," as the residue was called, were combined with other casks' residues, and the new higher levels of spirits in the casks were more easily emptied through the valve in the cask's head. These end-of-the-cask spirits had particulates, dregs, in them and so were sold cheaper than the first pour from a new cask.

This blend of several casks' final drops through the spigot (cock) were cocktails. To the liquid was added sugars, water, or even flavorings, like fruit, to make them more palatable. The fact that it took over two hundred years to reach this explanation for an everyday and common word is not surprising. As noted earlier, these were busy times, and the name for a minor beverage development was not something deemed worthy of recording or newspaper space.

This circumstance was made all the more understandable when one considers that in that era, any drinks composed of multiple ingredients did not have proper names. Today a mixologist combines five ingredients, and before the final shake, a name is attached to the new concoction. Not so in the seventeenth and eighteenth centuries. Naming a drink was not considered necessary. Or it was considered arrogant. Or it was a "what's the point?" sort of exercise.

First of all, a drink composed of several disparate ingredients was not the norm. A drink was a single spirit or a wine or a malt beverage. Putting something else into the glass was not "a thing." Why would any public house proprietor do that? And if they did, why would the neighboring tavern copy the exercise?

The way the product came from the manufacturer was perfectly fine. The patron liked the flavors of the beverage, and the innkeeper was not about to fool with success while adding to the workload. Who would do such a thing? Even if it seemed like an innovative and good idea, the establishment would have to charge more for the service. And that likely would price them out of the market when compared with the costs charged by the tavern down the block.

Besides, if Tavern A came up with a drink, it was proprietary. If Tavern B wished to also have a drink featured at its place, then so be it. Those drinks did not need names. They needed tavern proprietors only. If drinking habits were changing, the rate of change was proceeding at a snail's pace. The drinking public was not clamoring for anything different than what they had enjoyed all their lives, as had their family's previous generations. Still, the times were indeed changing, with civil unrest and the age of steam coming together to alter the desires of the drinking public.

CHAPTER TWO

New Freedoms, New Traditions

The dawning of a new age is never a "this very moment" kind of event. Technological changes evolve, followed by early adaptors assimilating the outpouring of societal alterations, and then society as a group joins in. Such was the development of engines that were powered by the vapor from heated water: steam. As far back as 1125, a steam organ was at work in the great cathedral in Reims, France. And yet, while inventors could envision steam making hard tasks easier, the practicality of producing machines that could do the work previously assigned to natural elements or to strong human backs evolved relatively slowly.

Steam-powered private modes of transportation were deemed frivolous, and the construction was bulky, with the boiler and a series of pipes all working under pressure. Besides, everyone owned a horse, and families all had carriages pulled by horses or mules, so where was the "convenience" benefit? The distance between point A and point B was relatively close, and thus using steam was not thought necessary or advantageous.

Steam engines in boats seemed to provide the best benefit to long-distance transportation and to moving goods. Boats were at the mercy of the natural movement of water, downhill normally, and tides and winds presented impediments and led to unreliable scheduling for departures and arrivals. A ship, its crew, passengers, and cargo could languish with no forward progress, causing economic losses and missed commercial opportunities. Regular transportation up mighty rivers, like the Mississippi, was not a usual possibility.

In sending materials to market, barge companies in the American Midwest did not plan on reusing the shipping vessel. The barge was loaded with goods and freight in river ports in Pennsylvania, Ohio, or Kentucky; sent to New Orleans for reloading onto larger ships bound for world ports; and then disassembled after one use as a barge, with the wood going to construct homes and the rock ballast being repurposed for street construction in New Orleans.

Steam changed that dynamic, and now vessels could travel with some ease both inbound and outbound. That new ease of movement translated to more widespread travel habits of the general population. Distances between places shrank in terms of the time devoted for travel. And more people were now taking advantage. In this way, the steam engine was not necessarily the vehicle for the journey but was the mind-changing modern convenience that brought about a reassessment of the possibilities.

When that happened, stopping by a public house for a refreshment was not the simple act it previously had been. Before the middle 1800s, neighborhood taverns usually had been aware of a patron's desires and preferences in drinking and even dining choices. Drinks did not require names. "Oh, here you go, John, your favorite." But when America's wanderlust was encouraged with easier travel, those drinks and dishes had to be named, and there had to be some general agreement about the contents of the named beverage, all understood and agreed upon by proprietors, bartenders, and new customers. In this era of people moving about, it was the only way to assure that the patron was getting what was being requested. There were, of course, variations on a theme, but naming a drink gave everyone an idea of a starting point.

The new travel freedoms did not just apply to travel from town to town. The general public began to understand that there were places in their own town with which they were not familiar. Curiosity was awakened, and interest in discovering new dining and drinking establishments was enkindled. So naming drinks and dishes made it easier for new patrons to understand the language of a meal or a refreshment in a new place.

CHAPTER THREE

Emergence of a Classic

THE FIRST SAZERAC

2 oz. Cognac

½ oz. absinthe
(a later addition to the mix)

½ oz. simple syrup

3 dashes Peychaud's bitters

The Sazerac was one of the earliest cocktails to benefit from a unique name and a defined construction process. The first Sazerac cocktail was a combination of brandy (in this case, specifically Cognac), absinthe (but not in the beginning), sugar, and bitters, all put together in a particular and defined fashion.

Back in the 1800s, as today, many styles of every spirit and liqueur existed. The companies that manufactured those products had their own business-operating preferences. Many champagne houses carved out markets far from home and concentrated sales efforts in those markets. Moët et Chandon and Veuve Clicquot defined markets in northern Europe and even in Russia, where they established strong sales and product distribution organizations away from the motherhouse. In this way, the houses would not directly compete, and a "gentleman's agreement" would be honored so as not to waste precious sales resources against entrenched competition long distances from manufacturing facilities in another country.

Cooler climates made sense to champagne makers because the closer their products got to the equator, the more chance there was of losing product because bottles could explode from the heat. There was also a greater chance of injury to handlers and customers alike from exploding glass bottles exposed to too much heat. Cooler places minimized that risk for champagne. The same access-to-market understandings also existed for another unique French adult beverage, Cognac. But Cognac had an advantage over champagne when it came to delivering to expatriates a desired taste of home. Cognac is a fortified wine. It has a high alcohol content and is stable, important for shipping to warmer markets, thanks to the process of distillation following fermentation.

In fermentation, which is the biological and chemical process by which wine is made, the resulting liquid continues to develop and age. The process of fermentation truly never ends even years after considerable changes have evolved in the wine. Distillation is a heating process, and the resulting liquid is "set" after desired outcomes have been achieved, with no more significant product development or deterioration during the passage of time before consumption. In short, wine can improve to a certain point and then begin to deteriorate. Spirits, for the most part, are stable, with very little further change occurring as they age.

During an aging period for spirits, the distilled liquid will pick up characteristics from the aging vessel, like a wooden barrel, but the liquid itself, on its own, will not change. If there are changes due to temperatures or time, they are quite slow and minimal. Cognac undergoes both manufacturing processes. Cognac is a grape-based product, and the fruit, which has a natural expression of yeast on the skin, undergoes fermentation, converting sugars in the fruit to alcohol, in the same way all wines are created. Then the resulting wine is distilled, using heat to further advance the alcohol and the sugars into a spirit, which intensifies the aromas and the flavors.

The full story of Cognac, told very well on websites such as Cognac.com and in Dale DeGroff's *The Craft of the Cocktail*, is the perfect liquid example of necessity meeting demand. For each Cognac house, establishing the product in a market entailed another important factor besides the delivery of a solid product to those wanting the experience: cost. Transporting large quantities of liquor to a market that was months away by ship involved considerable risk and effort, so it was not a cheap proposition to deliver a bottle of Cognac from France to the New World. Sazerac de Forge et Fils Cognac, a family-owned and operated business, focused its sales efforts on a new market, a French colony, La Nouvelle Orléans, on the coast of the Gulf of Mexico in a still-forming United States. The Cognac house likely predated 1800, but the earliest release of the spirit has generally been defined as 1811. In order to release an 1811 vintage, it is likely the Sazerac house and its products dated back to 1800, at least.

There was a château, and there were vineyards. The style of Sazerac Cognac was pleasing, not complicated or overly fussy, and the widespread distribution into the New Orleans market made for a happy cocktail development. The Cognac was not too harsh or sweet, and it played well in the sandbox with bitters, absinthe, and sugars.

The Cognac also targeted with promotion and distribution other population centers of the United States, notably New York and Pittsburgh, as well as larger ports along the East Coast. All of which presented the least complicated solutions to the transportation challenge, all great and thriving ports on major bodies of water close, relatively speaking, to Europe and the vineyards and châteaus of France.

There is some discussion among historians, including the much-respected Dave Wondrich and New Orleans cocktail historian and talented mixologist Chris McMillian, that Sazerac Cognac was not used in the original cocktail that bears its name, but I cannot verify its absence. It seems such speculation is based on the lack of contemporary affirmation in books or newspaper articles about the Sazerac cocktail. The lack of historical reference is presented as proof that the Sazerac Cognac spirit was not in the original recipe, and a certain group of influential writers have capitalized on the void. On the surface, to this writer, it makes no sense that a cocktail would be created and named after a brandy that is not present in the finished drink. It does not seem logical that a cocktail would take on the name of a real product without that product being present in the recipe.

To be sure, it is entirely possible that Sazerac Cognac was not the only Cognac used in the construction of the Sazerac cocktail. Sazerac was a favorite brand of the New Orleans population, but there were other brands that from time to time entered the market, and with hard sales work by their backers and investors, as well as pricing advantages, they moved into a favored position with consumers. But there seems no logical rationale, or historical proof, why a cocktail would take on the name of a specific spirit and then not include the spirit in the recipe, particularly at a time when naming a cocktail was something new to the population.

The role of Cognac in a French tippler's repertoire is undeniable. Here is one of the most specialized spirits to be found anywhere in the world. The beverage has to originate in a specific place, and it uses grapes that flourish in that place, and the manufacturing process is defined by French law. Creating a "new" cocktail that includes Cognac would be the ideal statement for French mixologists or pharmacists to honor their homeland, whether they were there in spirit or with feet on the ground in *la belle France.*

THE MYSTERY OF ABSINTHE

While the manufacture of absinthe was not confined to France, that country provided the backdrop for the most revered expressions, alongside Switzerland. Absinthe is a high-alcohol spirit, often as high as 62 percent alcohol by volume and more. Potent.

Amy Stewart, in *The Drunken Botanist,* notes that healthful, ubiquitous plants require little human influence to produce mind-altering results. In fact, oftentimes we cannot avoid plant life's influences on human behaviors. Absinthe serves as a prime example of putting a plant through a process and finding surprising and amazing outcomes. Absinthe is a new spirit by any definition. Its creation dates to the late 1700s in Switzerland. It has strong roots in medical and pharmaceutical traditions, with the inclusion of wormwood, one of the three herbs used in its production. Wormwood, an oddly named herb, was recognized by the Egyptians as far back as 1700 BC as a medicinal especially suited for stomach ailments. The bitter nature of the wormwood leaf was referenced as a basic taste sensation in the Bible and later, in the sixteenth and seventeenth centuries respectively, in the works of Shakespeare and John Locke. Wormwood possesses dominant flavors and aromas of anise. There is a green aspect to wormwood, and the plant has gained followers who hold the common belief that the plant has hallucinogenic powers. There is some minor truth to the thought, although the plant's ability to send users into fits of ecstasy or self-mutilation is greatly exaggerated. The other two herbs involved in the manufacture of absinthe, green anise and sweet fennel, both bring different properties to the creation of absinthe.

Absinthe, from the beginning, took on mythical attributes. It was, in fact, considered a very strange liquid and was always treated as such. There are two main aspects of absinthe that have given it its fabled status: a distillation process that yields a spirit of incredibly high alcohol proportions; and the presence of thujone, a menthol-odor ketone given credit for absinthe's psychedelic effects on the user. But thujone is not the oft-blamed culprit in stories of strange behavior or destructive actions by absinthe users. More likely, the high alcoholic content of absinthe can take the credit for rumors of absinthe-induced insanity, bodily mutilations, and strange mental visions that supposedly drive the absinthe drinker insane.

The actual case of absinthe, which has only been proven

recently by modern chemical testing methods, is that it contains relatively little thujone. The level of thujone present in absinthe could not reasonably be credited with any hallucinogenic events. Cutting off one's ear, as in the case of the talented painter Vincent van Gogh, was likely a result of the user desiring to make a strong public or personal statement about their own mental health rather than the effect of any outside influence, like imbibing absinthe. Depictions of the tortured artist were expected in creative types, and some personalities were only too happy to oblige the stereotype. Drinking spirits of incredibly high alcoholic volumes likely did not detract from the story about troubled creative personas.

Absinthe "bans" were probably more attributable to market influences between competing alcohol products rather than government efforts to protect the safety of the citizenry. Absinthe caused the user to become intoxicated faster than wines, beers, or other spirits, and in many cases was therefore desired by those members of society who were seeking a quicker escape from reality through external influences. When the absinthe drinker got "high" on absinthe, that usually was the end of the session, and then sleep was the cure. Not drinking other spirits was a likely and predictable outcome. And those spirit companies whose product was left on the shelf were not pleased with the lack of consumption, so outrageous stories of absinthe's hallucinogenic powers were created and enhanced.

During the staid Victorian age in Europe, the enjoyment of absinthe was divided into two camps. It appealed to a bohemian culture that was opposed by mainstream members of society. Liberal, arty types gravitated to absinthe for the revolution against society the spirit symbolized. Other segments were vehemently opposed to absinthe because of the association between free thinkers and its consumption and because of mercantile considerations: the use of absinthe detracted from the consumption of more usual forms of alcohol, such as wine, beer, and other spirits. Because there were no large manufacturing champions of absinthe, those influential and wealthy families who created more mainstream alcohol-based beverages had their way with legislation to ban a worthy competitor's products from the marketplace.

Before the bans, it was considered quite "modern" for mainstream citizens to demonstrate an enjoyment of absinthe. The statement that common folks wanted to make was to appear "with the times," very avant-garde. To be fair, there was also a large segment of the population during the 1700s and 1800s who were not happy with their lot in life. Their living conditions were not improving during a time when great strides in sociological conditions were taking place. Machines and modern innovations, such as cooking indoors, gas lighting, and indoor plumbing, were on the scene but not available to everyone. Misery was widespread, and those at the bottom of the economic scale continued to suffer with loss of employment, poverty while employed, more exposure to disease, and lack of respect from those higher up on the economic ladder. Absinthe appealed to these downtrodden elements of society as it was an effective and quick escape from reality.

The irony of absinthe was such that it also served the other side of polite society. It was quite accepted for even the well-to-do to imbibe absinthe. Such actions demonstrated an open-mindedness, a spirit of adventure to friends and associates. There was the tinge of danger along with the feelings of euphoria that followed absinthe's ingestion.

But the overwhelming bitterness of absinthe put off many potential patrons, so elaborate procedures and apparatus were created to make absinthe more enjoyable to "refined" palates. These procedures can be compared to today's rituals in the ingestion of certain chemicals and drugs. In the case of absinthe, expensive crystal bowls were created and placed on raised precious metal or glass stands. These bowls had multiple spigots along the bottom. Cold water was placed in the bowl, and a glass containing a little absinthe was positioned under each spigot. Then a little water from the bowl was dripped onto a spoon that was punctuated with multiple slots. A sugar cube was placed on the spoon, and the drops of water diluted the sugar, and the mixture then dripped through the slotted spoon into the absinthe in the glass. When the absinthe in the glass, with the cool water and the sugar, turned cloudy and slightly green, the drinker was ready to enjoy the results of the ritual. With multiple participants gathered 'round, the use of the absinthe fountain ensured conversation and conviviality. The ritual brought all participants socially closer together.

It was primarily the French, well versed in the distillation of absinthe, who adopted absinthe as a social outlet. Absinthe bars sprang up all over Paris and even in the New World, most notably New Orleans, a French community. The absinthe bar now known as the Olde Absinthe House was constructed at the corner of Bourbon and Bienville Streets in 1806. It was converted to a public house, the Alexis Coffee House, in 1846. It received its current name in 1874 in an attempt to be "hip" through association with the believed-to-be hallucinogenic liqueur.

There was always the desire to enjoy absinthe for what it could do to the body and the mind, but it was not the easiest spirit to imbibe. And it resulted in a level of intoxication that rendered the user sleepy or catatonic in short order. The ritual of the absinthe fountain, in the eyes of society, kept matters at a high level of discreet acceptability.

The Olde Absinthe House, ca. 1935. This is one of the oldest bars in New Orleans, on the corner of Bourbon Street and Bienville in the Vieux Carré. The current building was constructed in 1806, and the bottom floor was converted to a coffee house (bar) in 1815. Legend persists that during the War of 1812, Andrew Jackson met with privateer Jean Lafitte on the second floor to request his help in defending the city. Lafitte and his men assisted Jackson in defeating the British in the Battle of New Orleans in 1815. *The Historic New Orleans Collection, Acc. No. 1979.326.6.*

As cocktails became popular in both the Old and the New Worlds, a new outlet emerged for absinthe's enjoyment, and the social ritual of the absinthe fountain was no longer necessary to the communal drinkers of the times, the middle 1800s. It became simpler just to add a little absinthe to the cocktail, and the party continued. But not much absinthe is necessary to accomplish a good feeling or a change of taste. And there was still a desire for a ritual.

To this end, with the creation of the Sazerac cocktail, a little absinthe was placed into the mixing glass. The glass was then twirled in the air, tossed, in a spinning motion. The absinthe coated the inside of the drink's glass. Any excess absinthe, usually only a few drops, was discarded. Into the rocks glass containing the absinthe (¼ oz.), chilled, was placed a sugar cube, rye whiskey or Cognac (1½ oz.), and three dashes of Peychaud's bitters.

Some would say that Herbsaint Liqueur, created after the repeal of Prohibition, is a reasonable substitute for absinthe. Some would say that rye whiskey is a reasonable substitute for Cognac. Both suggestions have their proponents. And for a cocktail to remain close to its original design, with its original name intact, for more than 175 years, is quite an accomplishment. Unequaled in the adult spirits world.

437 Royal Street, now James H. Cohen Antique Gun shop, the former location of Peychaud's Pharmacy and Coffee Shop. About 1835–37, the pharmacist Antoine Amédée Peychaud created the secret recipe for Peychaud's bitters, a key ingredient in the Sazerac cocktail. *Photo by B. J. Rust, 2019.*

CHAPTER FOUR

The Pharmacist's Concoction

PEYCHAUD'S SUCCESS

In 1837 New Orleans, the pharmacist Antoine Amédée Peychaud was very good at what he did, and that was to concoct and dispense medicine created to cure specific ailments. His bitters creation, a secret recipe known only to him, either actually brought about desired results or appeared to accomplish the health goals of the user because the additive masked the terrible taste and smell of the medicines of the day. It did not hurt that bitters are usually close to 50 percent alcohol.

Peychaud's pharmacy, at what is now 437 Royal Street, around the corner from his apartment in the 700 block of St. Louis, flourished. His bitters, desired by the consuming public, were a word-of-mouth, taken-by-mouth pharmaceutical success. Many American investors, who were now literally flowing into the city, approached this talented man, wanting to assist him in expanding his business.

One of the ways Peychaud separated his practice from his competitors, and there were many, was touting a multitude of applications for his proprietary bitters product, including additions to coffee, culinary efforts, medicine, and a "new" direction—cocktails. For a while during the 1840s, it was perfectly acceptable to serve the new Sazerac cocktail in Peychaud's apothecary. While the delusion of a medicinal concoction was appreciated by businessmen and dockworkers, the social aspects of the beverage soon overtook the refreshment's main purpose. Its use very likely continued behind the veil of medicine, though more likely the gatherings in Peychaud's apothecary were excuses for back-fence gossip sessions and sharing news of the day, all encouraged by the high alcohol content of the bitters.

By 1853, Peychaud was making more income from bitters than from his pharmaceutical services, and by 1855, he had moved to larger quarters at 108 Royal Street, closer to Canal Street. This move was first noted in a newspaper advertisement appearing in the *New Orleans Daily Picayune.* On July 9, 1857, another paid advertisement appeared in the same newspaper and was headlined "American Aromatic Bitter Cordial." It states:

> This Cordial, whose delicate flavor and aroma are unsurpassed, is the most successful tonic and restorative known in cases of general debility: it restores the appetite, invigorates the action and functions of the stomach, and thereby prevents dyspepsia, so often brought on by continued attacks of indigestion, the prevalent complaint of hot and humid climates. Said Cordial may be administered with equal efficiency to the infant and the aged, by following the directions printed on the label of each bottle; and its agreeable taste is not the least of its recommendations. This Cordial has been introduced into general use in the Sazarac House and other principal Coffee houses in this city, as far superior to Boker's Stomach Bitters, so cele-

brated throughout the United States; and there can be no doubt that all who have tasted the AMERICAN CORDIAL, give it the preference over all other bitters in use. A. A. PEYCHAUD, *108 Royal street.*

Note the reference to the Sazerac House, and note the reference not to a medication but to a "cordial." Here was a connection between place, ingredients, preparations, and consumer use.

The ad was an attempt at what was obviously a public education campaign about bitters. Peychaud likely was seeking ways to survive, and he embarked on an aggressive advertising campaign featuring the Sazerac cocktail and his bitters. The effort encouraged other bar operators to adopt Peychaud's bitters and his recipes in their offerings. This communications effort further established the Sazerac cocktail as the "gold standard" of mixed adult drinks.

Even with the advertising, however, bitters remained the mysterious ingredient in cocktail recipes, medications, and even some food preparation. Peychaud followed the dictum of modern marketers: expand the use of the product beyond its original applications. Subsequent newspaper advertisements from Peychaud, all of which appeared between 1855 and 1859, were titled *Just in Time, A Really Good Thing, A Word or Two about Bitters, A Dialogue,* and *The Only Real Bitters.* Peychaud's business did not thrive, and it did not fail. By 1860, the city directory lists his businesses at 90 Royal Street and 108 Royal Street. Peychaud did bring in investing partners to the new outlets. Along the way, he was able to provide employment for two of his children and also had in his possession two slaves.

Peychaud's bitters is still considered the zenith of bitters products and essential, according to cocktail experts,

Newspaper advertisement, about 1860, for Peychaud's bitters.

in the making of a proper Sazerac cocktail. To be sure, bitters remain an enigma to this day. While bitters manufacturers and conjurers will tell you their product is in the recipe, they will never divulge what herbs and spices are in their bitters. Some bitters products are dominated by a particular food item, usually a botanical or an herb, but the percentage of the ingredients is never disclosed.

CHAPTER FIVE

New Players in New Places

Sewell Taylor arrived in New Orleans in 1838, likely having come from Pensacola, Florida, where he and his brother Edward operated a hotel. In the early 1840s, they opened the Merchants Exchange Coffee House on Exchange Alley in the French Quarter, in competition with Peychaud's operation just a few blocks away. Drinking parlors, even with hard spirits, were euphemistically known as "coffeehouses," and there were many throughout the neighborhoods of New Orleans, serving both coffee and alcoholic cocktails.

In 1852, Taylor lost his lease and decided to step away from the day-to-day running of the coffeehouse and concentrate on importing liquor from France, including Sazerac de Forge et Fils Cognac. He created a full line of ready-to-drink Cognacs and cordials, all labeled with the Sazerac moniker. The new manager of Merchants, Aaron Bird, changed the shop to focus on more profitable items, including cocktails and coffee, and the shop was renamed the Sazerac Coffee House. It was now located next door to the former Merchants Coffee Exchange and had entrances from Royal Street and Exchange Alley. It was immediately a commercial success, featuring the full line of Sazerac brandies, in addition to cocktails. This destination oasis had a bar that could accommodate twelve people—behind the bar. All of them spent their days concocting and mixing Sazerac cocktails.

Opposite: The Historic Exchange Alley in New Orleans' French Quarter, created in 1831 as a back entrance to the Merchants Exchange. Its original name was Passage de la Bourse. One of the coffee shops along the alley was the infamous Merchants Exchange Coffee House, which also had an entrance on Royal Street. It was there that proprietor Sewell Taylor settled on Sazerac de Forge et Fils Cognac as the main ingredient in a Sazerac cocktail, along with Peychaud's bitters. Illustration dates from about 1900. *The Historic New Orleans Collection, The L. Kemper and Leila Moore Williams Founders Collection, Acc. No. 1950.39.*

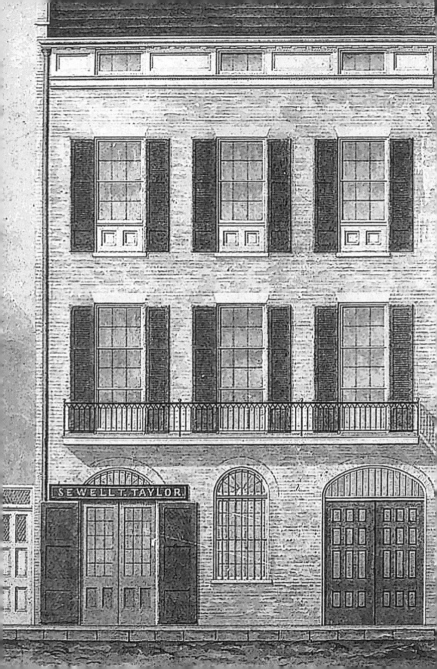

SEWELL T. TAYLOR

By this time, the Sazerac cocktail was ubiquitous. Many coffeehouses, bars, and restaurants were serving the beverage, and there was general agreement on the recipe and the process to make the drink. Such overall consistency of a drink was not the norm during this period in the development of cocktails, and it likely paved the way among professional servers for other same-name, same-recipe cocktails, like the manhattan, the old-fashioned, and the sidecar.

During the turmoil leading up to the Civil War and during the conflict itself, New Orleans, thanks to its prosperous port, economically held its own. Its residents had very little interest in the conflict, and many in the city did not even consider themselves Americans. The lingering influences of Europe in New Orleans were undeniable. French was spoken throughout the city, and to a lesser

Opposite: In 1860, Sewell Taylor established a wholesale distribution company directly across Royal Street from the coffeehouse he originally owned, the Merchants Exchange Coffee House. Taylor became the sole importer of Sazerac de Forge et Fils Cognac, among other spirits. *Courtesy New Orleans Notarial Archives.*

degree, Spanish was heard. In the early days of the war, there were local rumblings about maintaining trading partners with the North, but early on, Northern soldiers marched into New Orleans, claimed victory, and not a shot was fired.

The tempo of the community slowed down only when freight traffic on the Mississippi River was interrupted by the occasional military barricade or if there were battles upriver, making the shipping of goods treacherous. But denial was the order of the day, with the idea that the conflict would subside and life would return to a normal state.

The economic ravages of the Civil War and the loss of two sons in battle forced Peychaud to close his Royal Street pharmacy by 1869. But the bitters recipe, his main asset, lived on. An investor, H. J. Rivet, a wholesale and retail pharmaceutical manufacturer, was a partner in the Peychaud's bitters enterprise and financially supported making the bitters product.

In 1871, the Sazerac House, now named Sazerac Bar, moved across Canal Street to the American sector, to 300

Carondelet Street, at the corner of Gravier Street. That was where the new center of society was taking root, alongside a regrouping business community. Thomas Handy, who had begun as a clerk, was the manager of the Sazerac Bar and responsible for its new name.

In 1879, Rivet ran into economic hardships, and Handy soon owned the rights to the American aromatic bitters product. The product and the company did very well because it was an established and respected additive to many creations, specifically named as an ingredient in drinks and culinary creations.

THOS. H. HANDY,
IMPORTING AGENT,
Sazerac Brandies, Fine Wines and Liquors,
PEYCHAUD BITTERS, IMPORTED AND DOMESTIC CIGARS,
Nos. 9 and 11 St. CHARLES street, New Orleans.
myl'80—1yW5thp

Newspaper ad, ca. 1880, noting Thomas Handy as the wholesale agent for Sazerac products. By this time the company has moved across Canal Street to the American sector of New Orleans.

Newspaper ad for Sazerac cocktails from Thomas H. Handy & Co. Sazerac cocktails were premixed and sold ready-to-drink in the early 1900s. *Intern Ocean Sun, February, 17, 1901, 38.*

By the time of Peychaud's death, at age eighty, in 1883, there were a number of owners and managers involved with Sazerac House and Bar, both as a wholesale operation and as a retail supplier and consumer outlet of liquors. Yet there were ominous clouds on the winemaking horizon in France.

Sazerac Fizz

THE OLD TIMER SAYS "IT'S GOOD"

Here's a new palate tickler as good as the old time Sazerac drinks.

Of course it"s soft, but OH, so refreshing!

The New Soda Fount

Here you will find all your favorite beverages and a few mixed drinks you never thought of before.

OYSTERS

served at our Oyster Bar by Mr. Joe Pittari, formerly with H. C. Ramos, always fresh, ice cold and salty--direct from Bayou Cook.

SAZERAC
116 ROYAL ST.

Newspaper ad, about 1905, noting a variation on the Sazerac cocktail at the Sazerac Bar in the French Quarter.

PHYLLOXERA

A key ingredient of the Sazerac cocktail, in fact the core spirit that shared its name with the cocktail, was a Cognac, Sazerac de Forge et Fils. This spirit was especially well-liked in New Orleans and along the East Coast. Not a particularly high-end, high-cost spirit, it was enjoyed for its quality and cost. Sazerac was a true Cognac, hailing from the Charente region of western France, in the reasonably fertile fields surrounding the village of Cognac.

Agriculturally demanding grapevines would not do well in this region, but the Ugni Blanc grape does fit the requirements of Cognac. The grape is ideal for distillation, not so much as a standalone white wine. Ugni Blanc possesses good aging potential after distillation and pairs well, if necessary, with Colombard or Folle Blanche.

In the early part of the 1880s and through the turn of the twentieth century, throughout France there was a phylloxera epidemic. Phylloxera are very small lice that feed, in this case, on the roots and tendrils of grapevines. Phylloxera do not kill the vine immediately. Over a period of several years, they suck the plant dry of its vascular fluid, and the vine then produces less and less fruit each year, with declining quality along the way.

The phylloxera cure is to remove the diseased vines, destroy the plant material by burning it, and replant after allowing the field to lie fallow for at least three years. Considering that it takes a grapevine five years to bear quality winemaking fruit, there is an eight-year gap from vine destruction to a new harvest with completely new vines. The challenge becomes particularly acute with a wine with a long storage time, like Cognac. Even after a Cognac has gone through its legally required fermentation and then double distillation, there can be no product release to market for two years or more, depending on the quality designation level assigned by the château. During the late period of the nineteenth century, the challenge was exacerbated because replacing the vineyards had to be done all at the same time. The phylloxera epidemic was that strong and widespread. There was very little or no wine being produced in France, and that included the great wine-producing areas of Bordeaux and Burgundy, and Champagne to a lesser extent.

The effect on the marketplace was devastating, as the only grape products available were already on the market. Nothing new was following up. Many châteaus were forced to close their doors or take on new partners for financial support to get over the long period of destroying vines, purchasing new vines, replanting, and nurturing to first harvest.

With the Sazerac cocktail so firmly entrenched in New Orleans, the removal of a key ingredient, Sazerac Cognac, was a crippling blow. The "what to do" challenge was at the doorstep. New Orleans was, however, a prime port of transportation for Kentucky and Tennessee whiskies—notably rye whiskey. Here, literally already in town, was a key, well-liked, well-supported alcohol product that was found to make a very good substitute for Cognac.

Interestingly, the Sazerac family never objected to the use of their château's name in conjunction with a well-known cocktail that after 1885 did not use their Cognac. Granted, there were no big, splashy, national advertising campaigns, and the drink was mostly promoted on the premises of bars and restaurants, but such lack of action on the part of a copyright holder would not happen today. The story was made all the more interesting when in 1927 the copyright on Sazerac de Forge et Fils Cognac expired and was never renewed.

HISTORY REPEATS: ABSINTHE IS BANNED IN MANY COUNTRIES

The Sazerac cocktail lost another key ingredient to government edicts. Maybe. From its eighteenth-century beginning in Switzerland, absinthe always had a bit of a "bad boy" reputation. Its full acceptance into Parisian polite café society sealed the distilled spirit's reputation for being with the beautiful people at the right places. The user could have been the most conservative member of a banking family, but if a bohemian reputation was desired, the drinking of absinthe was sure to bring about the desired public face.

Absinthe, because of its greenish tint in the bottle, became known as "la fée verte," the green fairy. The embrace of this spirit on all levels of society, but particularly with the upper crust, was akin to American society's embrace of marijuana in the 1960s. While economic status was important, it was more important to show that you were a member of the "cool" group with the use of absinthe.

Patronizing a café devoted to the ingestion of absinthe demonstrated an acceptance and wide tolerance of all levels of society. Absinthe's reputation as a hallucinogenic-inducing agent was never debated or denied. And the user was expected to "go all the way," to a state of euphoria or, at the minimum, catatonic conditions. Merchants embraced absinthe's reputation as a drug, and they were only too happy to sell more product to consumers who were going to believe whatever they wanted to believe and who were anxious to demonstrate their liberal natures. If absinthe was good enough for the likes of Paul Gauguin,

Vincent van Gogh, and Edgar Allan Poe, then there must be something in the liquid that could bring about the artistry of more common members of society. Absinthe was enjoyed straight, such as in cafés with groups of pseudo-intellectuals gathered around an absinthe fountain, and the spirit entered mainstream society through its incorporation into the recipes for cocktails and culinary treats.

Absinthe took on qualities of legendary proportions. Users told stories of dreamlike apparitions, out-of-body experiences, gaps in memory, and performance of deeds that, upon sobering up, the user could not fathom. This bad seed image was used to sell more product, and the effects were never properly attributed to the very high alcohol content of the spirit. It was much more romantic to think the green fairy, containing thujone, had "drugged" the user. Again, absinthe distillers did nothing to dispel this notion of the presence of mind-altering drugs. This marketing falsehood would ultimately be the downfall of the product.

In the early twentieth century, there was a clash between producers of traditional products, like wine, and producers of distilled products, like absinthe. The wine-makers' vineyards, destroyed by phylloxera in the late 1800s, were now coming back and bearing very good fruit. But the alcohol-imbibing market had moved on to spirits.

After vast sums of money had been invested in replanting vineyards and then years passed waiting for the new vines to bring forth fruit, sales were at a standstill. Winemakers saw the core problem to be winning back consumers from absinthe. Wine drinkers liked the idea of a high-alcohol spirit taking them more quickly to where they wanted to go. Consumers were not going back to wine. The winemakers, who were some of the most famous and upper-crust members of society, were at a loss about how to combat a spirit that often registered at 64 percent alcohol by volume while their wines were at 14 percent.

The opportunity for winemakers came in August 1905, when Jean Lanfrey, an alcoholic Swiss farmer, spent a morning drinking wine and then at the end of his lunch had a glass of absinthe. In a completely inebriated mental state, Lanfrey murdered his pregnant wife and two children. The attention of the public was directed to absinthe as the culprit for this horrible crime, and from 1906 to 1910, most of the countries in Europe and the United States banned absinthe production and sales. The bans were accepted as the laws of the land, but in just about every case, the legislation contained errors of definition about how much thujone was allowed into the marketed product.

It was understood by all involved that the international ban on the manufacture of absinthe was real and in effect. That circumstance left many users, and the entire cocktail service industry, without an important ingredient in their repertoire. Pastis, also a spirit with a strong anise character, and to a lesser extent ouzo were used as absinthe substitutes, but they did not deliver the depth of quality or character desired by end users and mixologists alike. Not surprisingly, cocktails that had formerly used absinthe as a key ingredient, like the Sazerac, declined in popularity.

But as fate would decree, the Sazerac still had another key trick to show the world. The loss of two significant ingredients would not be the end of this cocktail.

A SUBSTITUTE WORTHY OF THE ORIGINAL

During World War I, two New Orleans soldiers, J. Marion Legendre and Reginald Parker, spent time in Europe and were exposed to absinthe distillation. They could not get the idea out of their heads that something was needed to fill the void left by the ban on absinthe in Europe and the United States. On their return home to New Orleans, they worked to develop a product that contained no wormwood, getting them around any objections the federal government had to an absinthe-like product. What they could not get around was the fed's objection to the name they placed on the commercial product, Legendre Absinthe, following the repeal of Prohibition.

Making good use of their New Orleans French heritage, they renamed the cocktail additive Herbsaint. Not only was Herbsaint a name that made use of many of the letters in the word *absinthe,* but the word translated to "sacred herb"—a winner all the way around. Even today, with absinthe itself in full distribution, many mixologists and chefs prefer to use Herbsaint in drinks and recipes.

Billboard advertisement for Legendre Absinthe. Canal Street,
January 1934. *Courtesy Sazerac Company.*

THE REPEAL OF THE DARK AGE

The "noble experiment," a prohibition on commercial production and distribution of alcoholic products, went into effect in 1920 after the 1919 passage of the Eighteenth Amendment to the Constitution of the United States. The Volstead Act, named after its main sponsor, Congressman Andrew Volstead from Minnesota, provided enforcement for the amendment. To his credit, President Woodrow Wilson vetoed the original legislation, but Congress overrode the president's veto, such was the power of the grassroots anti-alcohol movement.

Predictions of lawlessness, crime, turf wars, and violence went unheeded as the powerful and righteous anti-alcohol movement, led by the Woman's Christian Temperance Union in conjunction with the Anti-Saloon League,

Opposite: Pictured are the key ingredients used in making a contemporary Sazerac cocktail: rye whiskey, usually Sazerac brand or Old Overholt Rye, Herbsaint anise-flavored liqueur or absinthe, Peychaud's Aromatic Cocktail Bitters, and a sugar cube. Also pictured are a rocks glass, a lemon twist to rim the glass, and a long-handled cocktail stirring spoon. *Courtesy Sazerac Company.*

took hold of a country intent on recovery from a devastating world war in Europe. Prohibition, as the overall movement was named, brought about the rise of organized crime in America, forcing law-abiding citizens to break a federal law if not all the time at least some of the time, and an increase in deaths due to unregulated products that ultimately were poisonous to the user.

Ordinary citizens were overnight turned into outlaws, while many took advantage of the loophole in the law that allowed production of alcoholic beverages for families. Local governments found themselves in economic straits with the absence of revenues from alcohol taxes. At a time when law enforcement was particularly needed, there was little or no money in city or state coffers for equipment or salaries for police.

The criminal gangs who took over the production and distribution of alcohol became rich and were able to influence underpaid government enforcement personnel. This new public dynamic soon disheartened well-meaning citizens about a prohibition on alcoholic beverages, but corrections were difficult because the law had been made part of the U.S. Constitution. There was the additional dynamic that the criminal element was reluctant to give up its newfound and lucrative industry. Besides the manufacture and distribution of alcoholic products, those operating outside the law branched out and opened saloons and nightclubs to quench the thirst of an increasingly uncomfortable public.

By the early 1930s, the country's tolerance for outlaw gang violence had reached the point of no more, and the emotions of the preceding anti-alcohol movement had waned. In 1933, Congress passed the Cullen-Harrison Act, which opened the door to low-alcohol beers, wines, and spirits. That year, Congress passed the Blaine Act, which led to the passage, also in 1933, of the Twenty-First Amendment, whose sole purpose was the repeal of the Eighteenth Amendment. Once again, America had a legal industry devoted to alcoholic beverages.

Yet there was a downside to the Prohibition experiment: many cocktails were lost, and there was no further interest among customers to look back and resurrect previous favorites. Fighting a great war and then living through

Prohibition, during which time the Great Depression was upon the land, had lingering effects on the landscape and the people. The Sazerac was luckier than most cocktails. In 1949, the Roosevelt Hotel in New Orleans renamed its destination watering hole, located off its grand lobby, the Sazerac Bar. The hotel had purchased the rights to that name in 1948. The hotel's bar opened initially after Prohibition, in 1938. It featured wood paneling made of African mahogany and murals by famed artist Paul Ninas, both very much still a part of the décor. While most certainly not invented there, the Sazerac cocktail remained on the minds and lips of consumers thanks to the bar's locale, so prominent to residents and visitors.

Opposite: The Roosevelt Hotel entered into a naming and operating agreement with the Sazerac Company in 1948. This ad from the late 1940s made two important announcements. First, the Roosevelt's watering hole was now officially designated the Sazerac Bar. Second, in a break with the tradition of the original Sazerac Bar as a men's-only establishment, ladies were welcome every day. *Courtesy Sazerac Company. Used by permission of the Roosevelt Hotel.*

Sazerac Bar menu, ca. 1950, and the bar's official Sazerac cocktail glass, which can still be purchased as a souvenir. *Courtesy Sazerac Company. Used by permission of the Roosevelt Hotel.*

The Sazerac Bar in the Roosevelt Hotel had an outside entrance on Baronne Street prior to 1959, when design changes were made so that the bar could be accessed only from the hotel lobby. *The Charles L. Franck Studio Collection at The Historic New Orleans Collection, Acc. No. 1979.325.4594.*

Newspaper and magazine ad, ca. 1950. *Courtesy Sazerac Company. Used by permission of the Roosevelt Hotel.*

CHAPTER SIX

Renaissance of a Classic

After World War II and all through a period of Pax Americana into the middle 1960s, elaborately designed and produced cocktails were not in much favor among lovers of spirits combinations. Three-ingredients-or-less cocktails ruled the day. Gin and tonic, highballs, scotch and soda, bourbon and Coke, were all quite popular. Easily and quickly made, with a lot of room for measurement errors, these relatively simple offerings satisfied the cocktail-consuming public very well.

In the early 1970s, a new appreciation for sophistication began to take hold. Restaurants and bars competed for attention with extensive menus featuring elaborate preparations. Interior designs were also emphasized. Consumer service from attentive staff required training, and entry fees or memberships became common.

Foremost among this new breed of gathering places were the Playboy Clubs. Placed in key cities all over America, these destination watering holes and restaurants provided members with attractive women serving elaborate cocktails, fine dining, and entertainment, all in one location, with specific rooms for specific purposes, giving the patron many choices under the same roof.

The advent of private clubs challenged nonexclusive outlets to pick up their game. Soon a whole new genre of options appeared, all with the express purpose of attracting high-end patrons to drinking cocktails and enjoying gourmet fare. While these establishments operated at the top end of the economic market, businesses farther down the "food chain," in order to compete, also became destinations. And while that was playing out, the patrons themselves became knowledgeable and more demanding. Certainly, fine dining was the catalyst for this movement, but owners and proprietors soon recognized the importance of the bar and its potential for earning more profits. More high-quality ingredients, more elaborate preparations, and more attention to presentation were all hallmarks of the new beverage scene.

Once again, the Sazerac cocktail entered the fray. A winning drink on all fronts, it also brought a romantic and long history that the new breed of mixologist reveled in telling. By this time, however, the long ban on a key Sazerac ingredient, absinthe, had ended. Ironically, the blame for absinthe's bad boy, thujone, was the entry point for the liquor's return to commerce. Modern techniques of gas chromatography and other esoteric tests bore out the scientific proof that absinthe was not at its core a hallucinogenic drug whose effects were the result of a chemical ingredient in wormwood; rather, absinthe was a potent spirit that contained a high dose of alcohol. Thanks mostly to poorly written legislation in the early 1900s, no new laws had to be passed nor old ones rewritten for absinthe to once again take its rightful place on the back bar.

This drinking revolution was not just a blast from the

past. It was traceable to a true beginning place and a true patriot who led the masses away from cheap and artificial products to a genuine and delicious one.

REBIRTH AND RESPECT

The Rainbow Room, located on the sixty-fifth floor of 30 Rockefeller Center in the heart of Manhattan, opened in 1934 and from the beginning was considered a major destination for businesspeople and visitors alike. Because of World War II and the subsequent economic struggles of New York City, the Rainbow Room closed off and on until 1985. That year, owner David Rockefeller commissioned a total restoration of the space to its former glory based on designs dating back to its opening.

Bar and restaurant impresario Joe Baum was brought in to carry out Rockefeller's hopes of the Rainbow Room taking its rightful place among New York's many excellent culinary destinations. Baum, however, was also committed to another aspect of a successful public house operation:

the beverage program. Baum brought in a young mixologist who soon set the entire program on an amazing path. Dale DeGroff, a native of Rhode Island, joined Baum in New York City with the understanding that the drinks program at the Rainbow Room had to make the same quality and impressive statement as the interior design, the service, and the culinary offerings.

It was from this pulpit that DeGroff changed the face of American drinking. His methods and standards were considered groundbreaking; they are now the norm. His first book, *Craft of the Cocktail,* published in 2002, is regarded as the first guide to modern mixology. The book was soon referred to as the bible of the industry, and its recipes and tenets (always use fresh citrus and fruit, for example, never mixes) are as much a part of concocting cocktails as shakers and bar spoons. DeGroff took on the moniker "King Cocktail." He was awarded the coveted James Beard Award in 2009 as the Outstanding Wine and Spirits Professional in America.

DeGroff demonstrated his affection for New Orleans by founding the Museum of the American Cocktail there in 2004. After Hurricane Katrina forced a temporary move, the museum was welcomed back in 2008, the same year that the Louisiana Legislature proclaimed the Sazerac the official cocktail of New Orleans. Since 2014, the Museum of the American Cocktail has been part of the Southern Food and Beverage Museum in New Orleans. Because the Sazerac is so well-defined in terms of ingredients and processes for its construction, without DeGroff's heavy influence, the cocktail might not have enjoyed a proper rebirth respecting its origins and history. Mixologists everywhere were now dedicated to doing their craft right.

New Orleans also hosts the annual Tales of the Cocktail convention, attended by mixologists, executives from large spirits companies, and dedicated amateurs. Tales has taken its place among must-do experiences for those involved with the preservation and expansion of quality adult beverages. With the assistance of industry developments and events in the early part of the twenty-first century, the Sazerac was officially back to being an important cocktail in the pantheon of American drinks.

AN EXCLAMATION POINT

The Sazerac Company, based in New Orleans, is the nation's largest multi-label distilling company. In 2019, the company opened the Sazerac House, likely the most complete and intensive museum dedicated to a cocktail anywhere in the world, offering education in and experience of finely crafted cocktails, all under the banner of the Sazerac. Located in the 500 block of New Orleans's main commercial street, Canal, the museum has brought back into commerce a five-story building constructed in 1860.

Its forty-eight thousand square feet of space tell the story of New Orleans, distilling, and how products move to market. Guests can stroll through the museum and explore the many aspects of adult beverages. Included are an impressive array of interactive experiences, a working distillery, and multiple tasting stations to ensure the visitor appreciates the products' place in life's enjoyment. The Sazerac Company owns *Mr. Boston: Official Bartender's Guide,* the definitive cocktail reference, so questions about

The Sazerac House, Canal Street at Magazine Street. The museum contains a demonstration and working distillery, a bottling line for products including Sazerac rye and Peychaud's bitters. Interactive displays give details on the history of New Orleans and its cocktails. There are also virtual mixologists. *Courtesy Sazerac Company.*

ingredients and styles of any cocktail can be answered quickly through a computer interface, allowing the user to send the correct response to a personal email account. The company also produces Peychaud bitters, which is bottled on-site, along with Sazerac rye whiskey. As important to the Sazerac House visitor experience as product knowledge, the historical aspect about how products came to be

Bottling line, Sazerac House. *Courtesy Sazerac Company.*

and the age in which they were created is not to be short-changed or glossed over.

Another significant development in the long history of the Sazerac cocktail is the Sazerac Company's real estate purchases in the Cognac region of France. While the company was not able to buy the château where the Sazerac family has lived for more than fifteen generations, it did purchase a neighboring château and the original vineyards that produced Sazerac de Forge et Fils Cognac in the

1800s. These purchases mean that the brand name Sazerac Cognac will return to commerce, and because the Sazerac Company is in possession of the original distillation standards, the "new" Sazerac Cognac will be very close, if not identical, in style and taste to what was used in the creation of the Sazerac cocktail in the middle 1800s. This development, coupled with the fact that the Sazerac Company owns Peychaud's bitters, means the original Sazerac cocktail can be re-created and enjoyed by twenty-first-century aficionados in just the same way nineteenth-century New Orleanians enjoyed the refreshing cocktail.

Opposite: Column distillation still, Sazerac House.
Courtesy Sazerac Company.

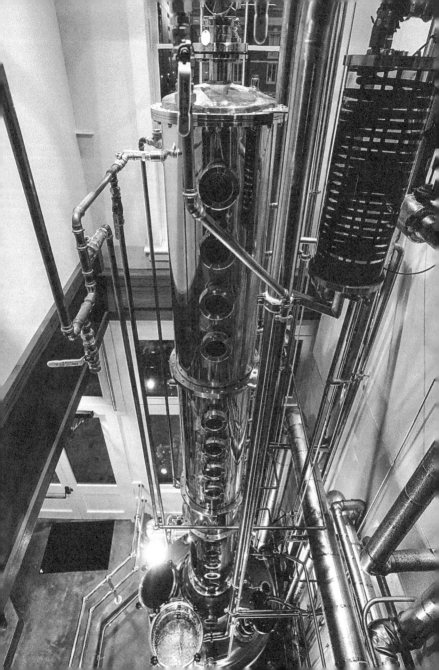

Ingredients used in construction of the modern Sazerac cocktail.
Courtesy Sazerac Company.

CHAPTER SEVEN

The Sincerest Compliment

RECIPES

Making a proper cocktail, especially a Sazerac, is the highest show of respect a mixologist can demonstrate to a patron. When the situation demands the finest, often it is not just ingredients but creativity, along with adherence to proven traditions, that takes center stage. Serving the drink with correct, high-quality ingredients, at the correct temperature, and paying attention to all of the traditional procedures are signs of talent and regard on the part of the mixologist and an extension of appreciation toward the drinker.

THE ORIGINAL SAZERAC

The original drink as created in New Orleans in the mid-1850s. Before that time, the Sazerac was a named cocktail but did not contain absinthe.

¼ oz. absinthe

1 sugar cube

1½ oz. Cognac

3 dashes Peychaud's bitters

Rinse a chilled old-fashioned glass with the absinthe. Add crushed ice and set it aside.

Stir the remaining ingredients over ice and set it aside.

Discard the ice and any excess absinthe from the prepared glass. Strain the drink into the glass.

Rim the serving glass with lemon peel and add the lemon peel to finished cocktail for garnish.

THE MODERN SAZERAC

The modern version likely entered the New Orleans cocktail scene around 1880.

1 cube sugar
1½ oz. (35ml) Sazerac Rye Whiskey
¼ oz. Pernod or pastis (after 1934, Herbsaint)
3 dashes Peychaud's bitters
Lemon peel

Pack an old-fashioned glass with ice.

In a second old-fashioned glass, place the sugar cube and add the Peychaud's bitters to it, then crush the sugar cube.

Add the Sazerac Rye Whiskey to the second glass containing the Peychaud's bitters and sugar.

Empty the ice from the first glass and coat the glass with the Pernod, pastis, or Herbsaint, then discard the remaining anise-flavored spirit.

Empty the whiskey-bitters-sugar mixture from the second glass into the first glass and garnish with lemon peel.

Many cocktails are actually "one-off" creations. The whole drink did not need to be reinvented, but rather, one ingredient might be changed through substitution or addition. And that one change made for a completely different outcome. These classic drinks are examples of minor variations of cocktails that came before. They seem different, and they are, with the outcomes going in a totally new direction but with only minor ingredient changes from previous much-loved classic cocktails.

OLD-FASHIONED

2 oz. whiskey (typically rye or bourbon)
½ oz. simple syrup
2 dashes bitters
1 twist orange peel
1 each Maraschino (brandied) cherry (optional)

Combine syrup and bitters in a mixing glass and stir to combine. Add whiskey, then ice. Stir. Strain into an old-fashioned glass or bucket with fresh ice. Garnish with an orange peel and (if preferred) a Maraschino cherry.

MANHATTAN

2 oz. bourbon

1 oz. sweet vermouth

2 dashes angostura bitters

Add all ingredients to a mixing glass and add ice. Stir to chill.
Strain and serve "up." Garnish with a brandied cherry.

As you will note, the old-fashioned and the manhattan
share a lot of the same ingredients. The old-fashioned is
the sweeter of the two drinks as it has sugar in its composition, while the manhattan uses sweet vermouth, which
makes for a drier cocktail. But the core ingredients are
along the lines of the composition of the Sazerac with, toward the finish, small changes to ingredients and how the
drinks are made.

A short word of caution: old-fashioneds are particularly
susceptible to the style of the mixologist. If you have a favorite construction technique or prefer certain ingredients,

you should let the mixologist know your preferences or be clear about how your drink will be made. You may be unhappy with the results if you don't communicate prior to service.

Thanks to Julia Tunstall in A Bar Above for the two preceding recipes and thoughts.

VIEUX CARRÉ

As created at the Hotel Monteleone, New Orleans, 1938. Here more ingredients are introduced to the Sazerac model but with incredible results and an amazing breadth of flavors. A favored local name for New Orleans's French Quarter, Vieux Carré translates to "Old Square." *Vieux Carré* is more accurate than *French Quarter* when applied to this neighborhood, New Orleans's oldest. The French Quarter is actually not French in architectural style but Spanish. After two devastating fires, in 1788 and again in 1794, the entire area had to be rebuilt. During that period, New Orleans was governed by Spain. Obviously, the rebuilding would reflect Spanish architectural values. The classic ironwork in the Quarter, still present today, is more akin to what is seen in Spain. The French style of ironwork is more straightforward and not so artistic.

¾ oz. rye whiskey

¾ oz. Cognac

¾ oz. sweet vermouth

1 bar spoon Bénédictine

2 dashes Peychaud's bitters

2 dashes Angostura bitters

Tools: mixing glass, bar spoon, strainer

Glass: old-fashioned

Garnish: lemon peel

Combine ingredients in a mixing glass and fill with ice. Stir well. Strain into an ice-filled old-fashioned glass. Garnish.

Recipe courtesy Hotel Monteleone.

ABSINTHE COCKTAIL

Other than a straight ingestion of absinthe, the absinthe cocktail may be the purest way to enjoy this spirit's many attributes. Dating to the 1880s, this cocktail was particularly popular in Paris as well as New Orleans.

1 oz. absinthe

1 oz. ice water (cold)

2 dashes anisette

2 dashes Angostura bitters

Pour the absinthe, anisette, and bitters into a cocktail shaker. Slowly add ice-cold water, then ice. Shake vigorously. Strain into a cocktail glass.

ABSINTHE FRAPPÉ

History tells us this cocktail, also known as the "Green Monster," was invented at the Olde Absinthe House by bartender Cayetano Ferrer in 1874. In 1843, a license to dispense liquor was issued to a coffeehouse, which was one of two types of government licenses issued for the service of alcohol in the town. This date is important because if it is true, and there are other variations on the history, then the Olde Absinthe House is the oldest bar in New Orleans still in operation. It is even possible that the Old Absinthe House was operating as a bar and a cabaret before that time, as contemporary newspaper articles have documented, but the first license to serve alcohol dates to 1843. Keep in mind that this being New Orleans, it is entirely likely that alcohol was served without a license long before 1843.

Ice, crushed and cubes

8 to 10 mint leaves, for muddling, plus a sprig of mint for garnish

1½ oz. absinthe

¼ to ½ oz. simple syrup

2 oz. club soda

Fill a highball glass with crushed ice. Muddle the mint leaves gently at the bottom of a cocktail shaker. Add the absinthe and the simple syrup (to taste), then fill with ice cubes. Shake vigorously for 10 to 20 seconds, then strain into the glass. Top with club soda; stir gently to combine. Garnish with a sprig of mint.

SOURCES

Baker, Phil. *The Book of Absinthe: A Cultural History.* New York: Grove Press, 2001.

Cognac.com—Everything Cognac website. https://www.cognac.com.

Cohen, Brad. "Everything You Know about Absinthe Is a Lie." *USA Today,* 10Best, June 6, 2018. https://www.10best.com/interests/drinks/everything-you-think-you-know-about-absinthe-is-a-dirty-lie/.

Conrad, Barnaby, III. *Absinthe: History in a Bottle.* San Francisco: Chronicle Books, 1988.

DeGroff, Dale. *The Craft of the Cocktail: Everything You Need to Know to Be a Master Bartender, with 500 Recipes.* New York: Clarkson Potter, 2002.

Felten, Eric. *How's Your Drink? Cocktails, Culture, and the Art of Drinking Well.* Chicago: Agate Surrey Books, 2007.

Haigh, Ted [Dr. Cocktail]. *Vintage Spirits and Forgotten Cocktails—From the Alamagoozlum to the Zombie and Beyond: 100 Rediscovered Recipes and the Stories behind Them.* Beverly, Mass.: Quarry Books, 2009.

Hess, Robert B. "Peychaud Bitters." *Drinkboy's Weblog.* Small Screen Network. Archived from the video podcast, June 13, 2008, and Sept. 29, 2017.

Miller, Anistatia, and Jared Brown. *Spirituous Journey: A History of Drink.* Bk. 2. London: Clearview, 2011.

"New Orleans Declares Sazerac Its Cocktail of Choice." *All Things Considered,* National Public Radio, June 26, 2008.

Regan, Gary "Gaz." *The Joy of Mixology: The Consummate Guide to the Bartender's Craft.* Rev. ed. 2003. Reprint, New York: Clarkson Potter, 2018.

Sazerac Company website. www.sazerachouse.com and www.sazerac.com.

Simon, Kate. *Absinthe Cocktails: 50 Ways to Mix with the Green Fairy.* San Francisco: Chronicle Books, 2011.

Stewart, Amy. *The Drunken Botanist: The Plants That Create the World's Great Drinks.* Chapel Hill, N.C.: Algonquin Books, 2013.

Thomas, Jerry. *The Bartender's Guide: How to Mix Drinks—A Bon Vivant's Companion.* Revised and introduced by David Wondrich. 1862. Reprint, Kansas City: Andrews McMeel, 2013.

Wondrich, David. *Imbibe! From Absinthe Cocktail to Whiskey Smash: A Salute in Stories and Drinks to "Professor" Jerry Thomas, Pioneer of the American Bar.* Updated and revised ed. New York: TarcherPerigee, 2015.